Mosaic Light

By Sarah Leo

Printed in Canada

First Printing, 2017

ISBN: 978-1-7751910-2-5

Sarah Leo
PO Box 507
Crofton, BC V0R 1R0

Dedicated to all those who've found light,
are looking for light, or have come to the realization that
they can be a light for others,
in all the beautiful and unique ways we are and exist to be,
gifts for one another.

Table of Contents

The Human Experience

SARAH LEO

Mosaic Humanity

We,
Are a beautiful mosaic of labels,
An ocean's depth of soul,
And a unique collection of dreams,
Yet to be.

Settings from the Inside and Out

Forest glades, surrounding trees and serenity ... deep within the
recesses of my mind...
Overlooking view, eagle-eye league and empowerment ... deep within
the recesses of my soul...
Moonlit lakes, mysterious reflection and inspiration ... deep within
the recesses of my sight...

This world, full of places, names and things; that are sometimes
unexplainable... where words can't describe their greatness... are
like moments of discovery, eureka moments that help Physicality,
join hands with Locality: to pursue those wide-awake-dreams...

Yet to be.

Midnight Magic

There's a mysterious beauty about the night,
Golden light illuminating the tips of trees and highlighting intricate
angles... all moving with ease... slowly, with control... swaying in the
soft summer's breeze... Like a stage light, shining a line-shaped
beam onto a 5-star show... I walk a little further and hear the echo
of steps merge with the flickering rustle of leaves... I look up to see
stars, vivid and silver against a deep blue sky...indigo in nature and
littered with dreams I imagine would connect my life like
constellations, around for centuries. The mysteries of the night, the
picturesque beauty captures my attention, and a connection I feel to
stars, and previous generations, also caught by this magic. It makes
me pause, wonder, dream, and feel inspired to experience the night
in a way that makes me wide awake.

Finding Home

I called: your name in the night.
I gathered: my belongings in the car.
I imagined: everything I missed.
I painted: picture thoughts of the map.
I walked: out the car towards the post office.
I said: sweet words to God above.
When I passed: my thoughts to other things,
I named: a time when we were closer.

SARAH LEO

Then I noticed: your car pull into the lot.
I stayed: transfixed by your presence.
I talked: to you for the first time in a while,
And I began: to realize the icebergs melted.
I arrived: at a place that felt like home,
In your gentle, full-bodied embrace.

I Want to Talk Without Words

I want to stare into the eyes of my best friend, and just feel love, to feel the warmth of his presence, next to mine, cross-legged and holding hands with a firm yet gentle grasp... Staring into his eyes sending inaudible messages... letting him know I care, without having to say it. To simply reach out and see him visibly relax. I want to slowly stand up with you, at the same time in your living room, and come together to dance, graceful, timid and electrifying slow movements, step after step... 1 2 3, pause, look up, 1 2 3 we both break into smiles, and 1 2 3 moving closer, over 1920s vinyl. I want to climb the trees with you, see the view and sunlit beams cascade over your frame, light illuminating the tips of your hair like gold, then climb down and watch the summer stars with you, at midnight in the grass, moonlight shining silver contours of the world with you, shadows tracing forest trees, and crickets singing in time for you. Running my hands through your hair, I feel the energy, see the brilliant colors radiating from your body, when you tell me your deepest hopes, wishes, and dreams for the future in a soft, and sincere yet strong voice. I could listen to you for hours, watching as your eyes light at the mention of life. I have so much love for you, so much compassion and a compelling draw towards you. You and your beautiful existence has crossed my path. For how long, I'm not sure; but I hope we get a good run for the time slots we are given...

Modes of Transportation

Surfing between rolling sun tunnels of sea.
Flying over miniature quilted maps of land.
Cycling through childhood memory streets reclaimed.
Driving to green light destinations unknown.
Skating around thin-ice topics,
But jogging past left-behind regret.
Skipping over chalk-covered stones.
Singing in full-city streets.
Laughing about thoughts of then,
So living life full steam ahead.

Chronology of Love

Keyhole light opens curiosity.
Walking through an old door,
I see my childhood self, at the beach,
Radiating soul.

Ocean roars,
Seagulls soar,
Life loops to an infinite bliss
As I held your kiss at age 22.

Doors slam,
Heart flutters,
Breathing gets tight
As I watch you leave, in the middle of the night.

Driving on, street lights rush past
Light then dark bright,
Before shadows I wonder about morality
But remember my remaining love
Strong enough to love again.

Jumping out of an airplane,
Air streaming past my smile
I think of life, how temporary it is and decide to live.

Childhood Fields

Tall grasses swaying
As wild as the crashing sea
Locate our adventure -
In a 1000 shades of green

As wild as the crashing sea
Wind storms through our hair
In a 1000 shades of green
I found you hide and seek

Wind storms through our hair
With cow bells in the distance
I found you hide and seek
Laughter giving you away

With cow bells in the distance
We crossed three acres of fence
Laughter giving you away
On your mark, we got set to go

We crossed three acres of fence
Exploring all seven seas
On your mark, we got set to go
Race, like lightning to the trees.

I Want to Know You

You know that moment,
When everything's aligned,
And the stars seem to shine?

SARAH LEO

Your expressions do that for me.
But am I searching or just observing?
I want to know you.
Walking along midnight lights after a show,
Walking with you anywhere just to talk,
Getting to know your words,
Hearing their vibrations,
Sensing the moments and places that give you joy,
Would be heaven.

I want to ask you about your dreams,
Under stars,
Feel at one with the moment,
Hearing crickets and watching shorelines on a driftwood log,
Being myself – nothing else,
Opening up to honesty...
Living and loving every second...
Staying true to the words dancing along my veins,
Like a highway to your heart.

I want to know the name of your pet,
Your favorite actor,
Sunrise or sunset,
Craziest thing you've ever done and wanted to do again...

I want to get to know the here and now,

But also your roots...
The intricate tapestry that is you,
All of the mountain views,
Instruments,
Small town stops, and cities,
The road trips,
Family ties,
Your stories to tell from the mic,
And moments of absolute silence that give you peace...
The person behind your name.

I want to sit on a bench in the fall,
Watch the old feed birds,
Make stories of their secret lives...

I want to see the painting,
The one where you brushed every color and detail of the scene.
What does it look like?
Are the strokes broad or gestural?
Thin with intricate lines...
Blue like the sea?
Or red like a sunset in a forest of autumn trees...
Did you start in the middle?
Or work yourself in from the sides...
A small voice in my heart asks,
...am I in it too?

SARAH LEO

Earth

Shifting, changing, turning gently
Growing, coloring, fading
Warming, cooling, atmosphere
Photographed, painted, created mass
Natural, industrial, jungle city
Earth,
A small glass marble in the universe,
Yet a massive network of connection...

Radiance

There's a beauty to watching sunny trees, through living room
doors,
I lay on a light purple couch with soft woolen sheets...
My black cat curls, in the crook of my arms,
Fine silky hair,
Nudging along my smile...
Hearing the purr,
I look up with a thought.
Light catching my eyes, gone from brown to now bright,
They're vibrant, with thoughts of you...
In childhood living rooms,
Golden dust swirls, like magical beams...

I remember:
Springing out the door,
And running past summer trees: a blur of green, blue and yellow,
Hearing your voice
I followed a path headed for the shore.
Birds soared above trees, silhouetted in light,
And under-growth moss glowed,
Like your bright musical laugh,
Illuminated by reflections of the sky and my love...
As childhood best friends,
We had an adventure – finding shells, driftwood scepters, colorful
beach glass shapes...
Then jumping in, we found ourselves.
Salt water soothed our souls.
A rebirth, emersion into bliss...with you...
In the sea, you turned to watch birds,
Swooping down and spiraling up the setting sun.
In this moment, beautiful colors reflected on your half-turned smile.
The expression in your eyes?
Breathtaking,
Full of joy and a deep appreciation for life.
Before the sea,
I reached to hold your hand,
And we stood in a beautiful, comfortable silence...
Just watching and feeling content.

SARAH LEO

Life Lines

Entrance – visceral birth
[Vivid discovery]
Childhood – quick laughs with tears
Youth – emotional wrecks
Adolescence – identity forming
Words – maze of connection
Poetry – from the heart
Sensations – effect life
Freedom – liberates minds
Contentment – in small things
Direction – soul searching on
Circulation – shared craft
Transformation – sure strides
Alignment – by destined stars
Quality – of gentleman
Passion – sparks at first glance
[Universal love]
Peace – is light like shoulder wings
Individuality – self made
Plans – life dreams ahead
Breathing – easier now
Meditation – creates flow state
Acceptance – of all of me
Focus – goals get closer

Infinite bliss – hands held together
Hardship – strains this heart
Passion held – healing on
Letters sent – ink words linger
Golden moments – sunset life
Wisdom – life recalled
Laughter – deepens love
Tears – sensing death
Connections – holding on
Grateful love – letting go
[Unshakable unbreakable love]
Exit.

At the School Dance

Tingling hands held,
Nervous, our beating hearts sound,
Drum beats and sonic melodies,
They mark this moment in time.
Feeling free to express,
Connect, and break dance with our thoughts,
To be dancing with you,
Is all the Utopia I need.

Filled with an energy,
We celebrate in style,

SARAH LEO

Failing to conceal our grins...
In sync and apart,
We dance.

Moving together,
We can't help but stare,
Transfixed by this glee, this curiosity...
Iris to iris, and heart to heart like a freeway language, sent without
words.
The night strobes on, lit with color and packed with other dancers.
In the beautiful, glowing gym... I felt changed.

Theories of Personal Expression [modelled after Jan Zwicky's
Theories of Personal Identity]

The long embrace;
the dried tears;
the chin down
grey loon who's become
the swan of swans.
The snow town,
a.k.a. the winter bliss,
those gloved held hands.
The trolley, the small talk
The walk; the carols
Four skates; the laughs

Catch my fall. The connection
Studying your fearless eyes.
The love letter, or red waves
Signed on my mirror, or my heart.
The light knocking on this window.
The dancing on that dock.
The telltale stars.

Head versus Heart

Here's the point:
The Head and Heart need to have a really good relationship, above all. In order to keep this good thing going, there needs to be some compromise of one or the other. The Head can't always get its way, and neither can the Heart. Balance is the key to having a long, healthy connection where things work out...Sometimes, what is needed is a break from head duties. That's when you gotta live a little, have fun, and color your life with good memories to last, but too much though – the whole system shuts down in excess. Now how about those tests we are given all throughout life? Sometimes we gotta rein it in and give responsibility to need rather than want. But as mentioned before – too much need and the system shuts down, this time becoming cold and calculated. Ladies, gentlemen, there is a reason why both Head and Heart crossed each other's paths on the journey of life... They were meant to be together. Fate only had one thing in mind and heart when it stayed up late devising a plan. Their

lives depend on together, and that means working with each other on both a personal and professional means. Why??? You might ask... Because each has something the other doesn't. The Heart has compassion the Head simply does not, and the Head has rationality the Heart never will. And on the other hand, they were never meant to argue, as one person shouldn't always carry the weight... communication needs to be open, cause while one keeps time with sound, enriching mind with excitement, love and compassion; the other makes sure it takes care in a snap-to-reality vitally protective kind of way. In this way, they should always consider each other's situation. When life calls for it, compromise on roles – maybe even alternate on duties within the week, have one take over with a 7 day shift work then switch... But even shift work can get tiresome and jeopardize the relationship... As fate would advise, never say no to the Heart or Mind, just make sure there's equal participation, because they were both born at the same time, smelled the same sea air, heard the same call for adventure, had the same urge to ↘ dive in deep, experience beautiful depths, blue illuminated by shimmering rays of light... In order to dive, you gotta listen to your Heart; in order to float, you gotta use your Head. Complements of and crafted in conjunction with, Heart and Mind.

Bus Stop Passenger #1: Regular in Transport

She walks in geometric stride,
Constantly on the go –

Stacked to the brim with plans,
Internal maps she's drawn towards,
By a sharp-edged clock –
Keeping her on time.
Some call her the Cube Woman,
Having many different sides,
All within the framework of her calculating mind.
She tries to live a smooth and
Angular type of life,
Seeking perfection and
A multifaceted perception,
But the world isn't flat -->
Hills and mountains create an uneven slope,
That she hopes to pave a road on one day,
With signs directing the lost—
To be a sign herself
For precision:
Is her way of life.

Revolution of the Mind

How do you start a revolution, peacefully?
To set things right,
Let the light of your muse direct,
See the beauty in the unique,
And feel the joy

An unconquerable summer in any winter that enters our lives is key.
To weather the storm,
Feel a sense of unity and elation,
Just in knowing we can make a difference,
Will bring forth a peace:
Unimagined, unbelievable, and undeniable –
Something pessimists will not see, yet... still comes true.
It all starts here,
In a heart beating words through a mind along veins and out the hands,
The same hands that write: inspiration.
Through the mind along veins and out the lips,
The same lips that speak: love,
Through the mind along veins and out the limbs,
The same limbs that dance in joy and celebration of this beautiful life.
This I perceive from the mind's eye.
The mind is a canvas,
The kind the sun shines through and projects onto life
Upon thought mixed with action...
Laying awake at night,
Lamp creating a soft dim glow on the room,
I think of what's to come,
Preparing to live it,
Give it my all,
And believe in the dreams
I keep inside my stride...
When I close my eyes,
All I can see is you, me, this reality and a sound narrating it all,

My sound,
A signature formed by notes on four beautifully structured lines.
On the road I walk,
I see flocks of black birds soar – my hope my freedom,
Hear forests of elm trees rustle – my peace my serenity,
And I know friends, family and relatives walk behind – my rock my strength.
On this road:
We are supported by a community of souls, either from close or afar.
That man on the bus,
That girl in class,
That cashier at your grocery store,
All acquaintances who appreciate who you are and who you continue to be.
Just know:
There will always be someone rooting for your success,
To break free of tall brick walls,
To jump higher upstairs through academia,
To walk confidently towards rather than away from dreams,
To feel beautiful without anyone holding a mirror,
And to hear a lion's roar in your mind
Every time that you want to love
But need the courage to open your heart first...
I say let's start this revolution, today.

SARAH LEO

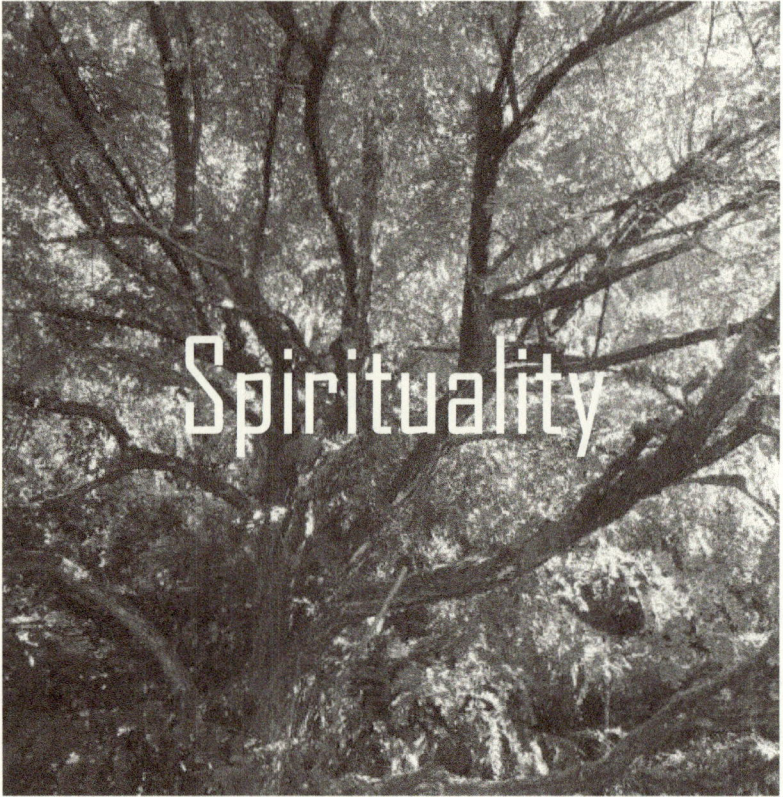

Spirituality

Communication

Words move around in disarray:
Jumping, flying, diving, falling, rolling, running on...
Like a circus in my mind.
Travelling on, the show must go on...
No matter the windstorm...
Even if it sweeps away words:
From underfoot,
Making me talk like I'm falling down stairs.
Sticks and stones love, but words can never hurt me?
It's a lie.
They can bruise and abuse like a nasty match of pain...
But suddenly, something changes...
A change flickers on the word UNLESS, and my world starts to glow
again.
Unless the words are not thrown...
But passed along instead,
They make beautiful shapes of flowers and suns, and pretty little
love notes that make me want to sing...
I can walk un-crutched, dusted off, and onto other things
Words so relieving and uplifting, my shoes grow wings
White and iridescent, soft and light...
Like a gift from God...because an angel came into my life and helped.
Holding doors with words –
Making me laugh with words –

SARAH LEO

And strengthening my stride with words –
You've walked the words you've talked, for me.
So for you my dear,
I will use the same, sweet-smelling words,
Show you the same open doors,
Make you laugh just as hard, and strengthen your stride at any
chance...
For you and others,
I will pass these words along,
For what always had the potential to be:
A beautiful, life, path.

A Beautiful Secret

Revealing secrets, caught between a mask, breathing to the sound
of your heart... this moment of discovery makes you feel exposed
and relieved... I can sense that to know and understand... to see the
world through your eyes... your hidden truth... is an honor. I need
you to know it makes me relate to your ways. I appreciate your
compassion. I am inspired by your courage to be unique. You've
found a way to see the unseen, to help those who fear what they
might see: by offering peace. By living this serenity and lending
words of advice, you're another one of God's angels.... Revealed to
my world, known for so long, and yet not in this way... this new truth,
I've been given an opportunity to know, makes me realize once

again: how amazing people can be... in the most unforeseen corners of this world.

Dedicated to an anonymous friend.

Advice from Random Heart Words

News flash:
Don't just wait for,
The weight of the world to rise off...
Just claim your hope,
Cause it'll spin you wings to soar past walls.

News *flash.*
You're standing at the altar of your dreams.
Mind full of color and winding paths to be,
When music fills your soul...
Do you dance or walk away?

Newsflash
My friends: The race is already won,
If you've followed your heart's direction!
That little voice inside,
Too polite to yell, to compassionate to stop
Whispering encouragement...
Reveals handy little sign posts to guide you near,

Destined... bus... stops.

Friends:
Like a reflective mosaic,
On the bottom of a sunlit pool,
The deeper you dive,
The more beauty you'll discover.
Irreplaceable vibrance within,
Simply glimmers from your eyes,
Every time that you choose to smile.

Inspiration & the Angels

Being inspired sets me free,
Liberated,
Powerful in my own means and at peace with serenity
To face whatever obstacles confront.
To see hard-set determination in people's eyes,
Expressions of perseverance in the face of terrible things...
To see the hope and humanity in their presence,
Steadying their balance, and slowing their stride to a powerful pace
Straight up hope, palpable strength... it's undeniable.
They are beautiful souls, walking out of hardship, smoke and debris,
Acknowledgment of the trial yet insistence on not remaining victim.
Preachers walk around street lights,

Delivering speeches: passionate, vivid, with a great sincerity and
gratitude
Of people who do and make beautiful things for the other,
Luminous angels of everyday life...
They take many forms...
The lady who smiled on the bus,
The man who held the door,
The child who described love...
They're with us,
Even in the hardest moments of our lives,
Their voices, muffled by the shouts of
War! Combat! Revenge!
But in silence...
When thoughts lay down to sleep,
Eyes becoming deep with calm,
Chimes resonate the air,
Their tones, lift morale,
When people make you laugh,
When a voice in the crowd says you're beautiful...
And when the nearest one inside your heart,
Echoes the very same words...
When intuition strikes
And an endless joy suddenly burns at the pit of your stomach,
Rising and blooming
Like a bouquet of flowers in light,
Fluttering... whispering songs of self-worth...

SARAH LEO

It all begins to make sense...
Then angels from higher altitudes descend to join the cause
Inspired by the everyday kind...
This subtle, yet euphoric process,
When you know you've met someone with hidden wings,
When you experience... the unexplainable joy and lightness after
mere words
I feel free,
Liberated,
Powerful in my own means and at peace with inner serenity
To face whatever obstacles confront.

What Would an Angel Do?

Acknowledge its wings,
Emit a vibrant, soft and glowing light on its skin from a dusty,
Shadow and light beamed church...
Experience bliss and divine acceptance for all,
And live with a full-bodied love for every aspect of you.

Find Your Light

Thinking, dreaming...
Pulling worlds, and starry planet speckled universes together.

Visions led awake.

This life is converging. Sky view looking down from great heights, gravel roads along desert paths, riding, gliding, wind rushing through hair, streaming, believing, on my way to achieving, the road of life I tracked. Co-created bliss, unity uncharted, yet preplanned amongst speckled stars. Universe responding through sunny wind whispers. Breathing in the air, expanding my lungs, arms outstretched, feeling adrenaline being captain of my soul in reverence to reveries creating light, spilling off sidewalks and under streetlamps. It lives to be seen, experienced, and loved in the blur of colored sun or the depths of hope reminded. On a cool autumn, gazing at life itself, realizing the light I see is the light I'm from.

It's meant to be shared.

<u>Heart Connected</u>

Fueling the vibe...familiarity, love, late-night bar conversations with unexpected wisdom shared. This is the good life, honoring those who pass, making their time memorable in the most meaningful way. This is our meaning, split into a million lovely pieces, one left for every time life changes for the better. I feel so whole, so content, a quiet yet feeling so full. Above all else, we need each other. We are gifts, blessings in disguise or apparent in sweet sincerity. Here's to fire-lit nights together, or in celebration of each other. Let us be there in hope, in voice, or in person for each other. Those still nights looking at stars, witnessing life's miracles.

The Bracelet

A thin black bracelet
Modestly adorned on my wrist.
Its only ornamentation a silver bead
Engraved "Imagine" on one side, and "Achieve" on the other.
This small token of encouragement,
Helps me to feel free
Of self-constructed walls.

To be lifted from all anxiety, resisting all pressure,
And standing determined walking confidently towards my finish line goals...
Overcoming adversity,
Narrates my story, with a dancer's poise,
And finds the "possible" in "impossible".

It's worked under stage lights,
In classroom desks,
And a few waiting room chairs where faith on wings, and a lion's courage: are required.

I've found a way to access strength,

And I'm constantly reminded,
The world I envision is only footsteps away,
As long as my lungs fill with air.

The sentiment dives in deep,
Plunging into depths of conscience,
Because it's given me all...
A treasure of invisible wealth,
In what looks like:
An elastic band with a single bead strung through.

My dad gave me this,
The day he left for work
It helps me picture his love and support,
And know a quiet power resides within my frame.
A reserve of energy... poised for action,
Flocks of faith... waiting to soar,
And a measure of confidence, ready to stand up and say:
Give your dreams a chance.

I look back to my bracelet,
Unwrapping its thin black lines,
Gently from my wrist,
And I know that I can do this...
Long after setting it aside for the night.

SARAH LEO

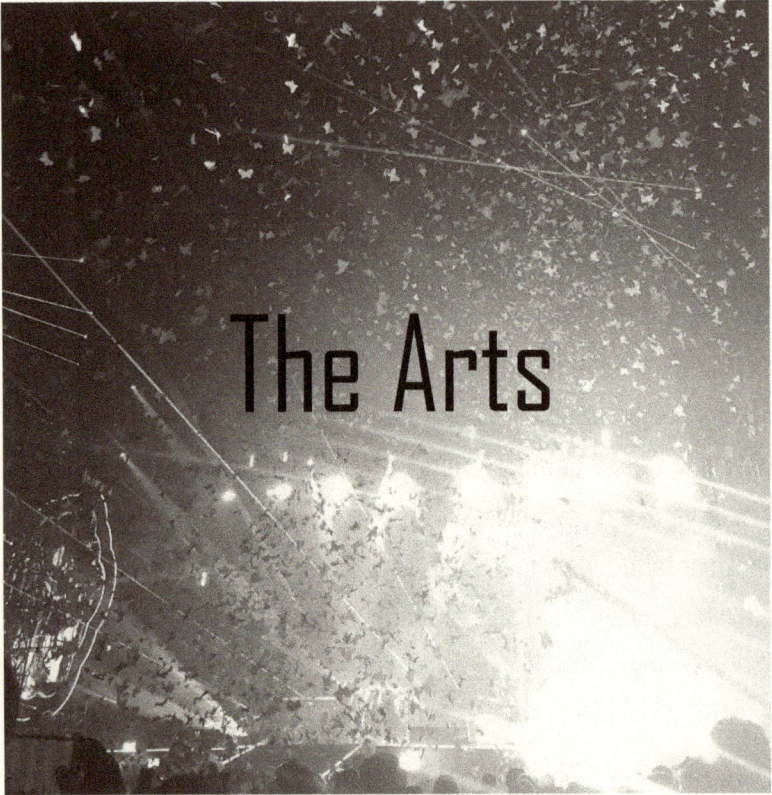

The Arts

Sight Reading & Singing

Sight reading musical Morse Code,
A language on the crosswalks of notation...
Walkingjumpingclimbing,
Decoding aerobics on and around the bars...
This speech is a leap through doors
Of an industry I crave...
Gaining expressive heights telling the world:
Things they need to hear,
Lines they need to keep inside their strides...
On a grander scale, this is the dream.
Sight singing...
Megaphone in hand,
Voice ready to see and create things never before seen or created...
To experience the thrill
Of understanding this code...
To speak it to others
Gives me a break in a room bathed in light,
Ringing with sound,
And melody lines only heaven could know.
This is my pursuit...
A musical one, to uplift a nation.

Taking Me There with Music

It's a concert in my mind, every time that I plug in to music, a beautiful sound emitting bass, tenor, soprano... In an indie rock song, a world of colored smoke machines, 100% honesty, and loud beats... most of which emanate from my core... Dancing to the song... rests are an eternity, off-beats jolt the senses, crescendos build with crowd-surfing excitement, and jumping casts all problems away... When people around you are feeling exactly the same... connection is marked and made as history... In my mind... Reflecting live shows to come and memorable ones past... A celebration of humanity... and all of our experiences live... To be one with music, people who love it and inspiring bands that make it happen with years of experience and a passion for the craft... they didn't let odds get in the way. Loving this life, and my three-minute song pulsing through earphones. Unity of bliss...

Dancing in the Now

Spinning round and around and around, laughing, with every movement aligned to this moment. Letting Freedom hit the stage and Hesitation exit through... no looking back. Vibrations of this energy from within reach out... Feeling at one with the music, expression, and a deep-set euphoria... these words bloom in the jungle of my mind... the span of three minutes grow into a lifetime, where poetry is in the arms, movement does not need words, and communication, the act of transmitting, transitioning and transforming thoughts... makes my heart beat. Lights, illuminate this radiant moment of contrast, where the brightness of my state turns the darkness of this stage into an indie-rock ballet, an animated walk down the street, a sea of adoring fans, a preview of the dream, and a readiness for it to manifest... Then a quiet moment of contemplation surfaces, where gratefulness creates strength that builds towers, and holds its ground with a confident foundation. It originates from my core and propels out my limbs... Using this frame, this rented physicality, my spirit can truly be honest. It sings, screams, speaks, laughs... with only a handheld recording, to account for sound... This feeling, this full-bodied bliss puts forth a dynamic set of steps, choreographed by the heart, and cryptic to the mind... A sincerity, so pure and full of passion that it fills the entire theatre room. The two-person audience stands curious and a little in awe, watching spontaneous movement abandon insecurity, and embrace exhilaration... Living in the moment makes me feel alive, beautiful... and loving every second: on the stage and before class starts.

Practice Room Hall

Walking through the hall
I hear trumpets to my right
Step with left, step with right
Walking through the hall
A piano's to my left

Step with left, step with right
Metronomes keeping time to the beat of my own drum.

It mixes as I wander through,
Step with left, step with right
Curious I hear a fusion of Jazz, Classical and Soul...
Looking in I see glimpses,
3Dimensional still-lifes of lives narrated by music.
Step with left, step with right

Travelling on...
I see an empty room with natural light through dusty white blinds.
Step with left, step with right
A Kawai Piano waits before me,
Curious as we are to hear each other's sound.
We stand, facing the other,
Caught by an overpowering urge to play
And yet,
I'm transfixed by the tick tock clock
Reminding me of a limited supply of hourglass sand.
Amount becoming smaller
As papers, calendars, and schedules fling through my mind

It was then that I made my decision.
I was going to live with carpe diem.

Music filled the small room with notes, sounds, keys, and
instruments playing
Sound on left, sound on right
And I felt whole, once more.

Soul Concert [modelled after Sia Furler's song *Lullaby*]

Hear the crowd roar like the shore,
Sea of hands rush up for more
Hear the crowd roar like the shore
Lyric love sounds from my core

Hear their heart beats drum as one
Connection resonates from fun
Hear the heart beats drum as one
Never alone my work is done

Cause when we sing
Wounds stop to sting
Reviving bliss
Your self-worth will never be a miss
Cause when we sing
Wounds stop to sting
Reviving bliss
Your self-worth will never be a miss

Hear the music feel the bass
We're strumming on the strings of life
So hear the music feel the bass
Your strength runs deep even in pain

Repeat this song in your mind
Whenever you're stuck to abide
Repeat this song in your mind
Recall for the brighter side

Cause when we sing
Wounds stop to sting
Reviving bliss
Your self-worth will never be a miss
Cause when we sing
Wounds stop to sting
Reviving bliss
Your self-worth will never be a miss

Hear the crowd roar like the shore
Hear the crowd roar like the shore

The Performance

The mind is a place to imagine, the canvas of coming events, and
experiences you'll have, in a sunlit existence that is warm,

incomparable & more beautiful than any other place of preparation. My fingers are tingling, and I'm getting that familiar feeling in my core, a fluttering heartbeat means:

I'm breaking free, throwing black curtains aside, feeling warm and colored light illuminate my soul, under it I feel alive. All eyes on this presence, owning the entire stage. I'm so free that life can take over without fear. Flow floods my mind. I make myself an orchestration of who I want and need to be. The words belonging claim the stage and beyond... I'm imagining my voice, travelling through the lives of every multicolored soul along different directions of life, like a network of paths, or a subway station map... Remembering this moment in time, the kind that blooms joy... I'm doing this for me. Voice rolling in, rushing like waves, my voice echoes to be heard, sharing my inner world with others in a pin-drop moment where all that matters is music, and the places it took us. To feel this music with every ounce of my core, honesty ripples through in ghostly shapes... glowing with invisible color. Thoughts take shape of their own accord and universal connection arrives. Before me, a sea of palpable notes, hopes and dreams collage, like a mosaic of humanity. Its presence is known... Becoming immersed in the lyrics, and telling this story from me to them, is pure euphoria.

I'm part of an outstanding group of individuals ready to share their heart and soul, and express what really goes on... We're in this together. It's no longer an us and them separation, but a fusion of recognition. You are part of this, as a beautiful, undefinable, and unique individual, with an energy so magnetic it's meant to be heard.

Love for a Musician

Slow down the clocks
Let me savor this moment...
Bask in its deep satisfaction
Brought to my entire core...
The sound of your voice...
Echoes through the room
Your beautiful song
Expresses my love perfectly.
In love with this moment for eternity.
Bon Iver, I'm in love with your sound...
Your contribution to the waking
Is the dream I've been waiting for...
In this time,
My ears hold a symphony of a three-minute utopia
Made by soft words,
Full of intensity,
Your expressions soar the wavelengths,
Carrying a message,
Glimmering and rolling, diving, gliding...
Energy many lives can hear...

I feel I'm surrounded in a cathedral of music, glowing with serenity
Invisible souls sit in pews
Filling the church with a love for all humanity
Coming out as your voice...
Bouncing off light-reflected walls,
Tall and full of doves
All flying in sync...
Also like your voice...
It soars...

Raises with soft grace
Onto the topmost window panes...
Then descending in a swirl of flapping wings,
Suddenly loud with a shift they glide up,
Then repeated waves applaud the air
Love More you say?
It's already done.

Listening To the Choir

Sitting in the pews,
All around me there is music from the choir,
In surround sound . . .

It is a seven-part harmony
And my heart beat in time.

SARAH LEO

Base notes vibrate *through* the floor,
Tenor lines move through my *core,*
And *soprano* notes fly into the air
Like birds,
Suddenly set free.

The music reminds me of love...
A satisfaction so pure
It makes my very lungs fill:
With anticipation.

Amber, red and brown leaves *waft* through my mind,
When lyrics bring me to a forest in the fall... and all of its windy
magic.
The music *lifts* in climax,
And rings true though the massive church hall...

The singers dress like Christmas ornaments,
Decorating the base of an organ which spans the *entire* length of wall,
And grows, as a majestic steel tree:
Up to sun-bathed ceiling beams...

The hall glows bright with stained glass color...
Steeping though windows, like a watercolor painting...
In the front row pews, all of the stage, organ pipes and ceiling:
Becomes an array of vibrant light.

The tone of the song reflects what I'm seeing,
And suddenly I realize
People can do *beautiful* things with air.
Turning silence into ringing,
And ease to intensity...

I was seven, and from that moment on
At sunset in a church:
I pictured myself singing, up there too.

Cultural, Artistic Beings

Everywhere I go, art reveals itself as daily life...
We all breathe, so we are all beautiful spectrums of life, whether we
are bittersweet, lead vibrantly euphoric lives or reflect, in the in-
between.
...As I pass a crowd of individuals, a mosaic of beautiful labels
innately sing,
Form glowing images above their heads and walk with
expressionistic intent.

What lines do you keep inside your stride?

Intrinsic mosaic heaps of life prevail and paint our world with
beautiful personality. What love, courage, and intelligence exist

within our comrades? Our neighbors collectively seen through rose-colored lenses are the most amazing entities around.

Sweet Dreams Perceive in Witnessing Dance

Sweet dreams perceive ... our heart's deepest desires.
He can feel it inside,
He can feel it command, pilot, control, and possess his limbs into
fantastic movements I will attempt to describe. Captivating,
entrancing, and engaging his beating heart — He doesn't take no for
an answer, failure is not an option, and nothing can stand in his
way... He's bulletproof from Hell and created for Paradise.

Where did it come from, what force is taking over, and inspiring his
soul to take flight? Something unworldly has given him wings. He's
frightened by the power he's releasing from within, but everything
inside of him is linked... and united, dying to react with a passion to
perform.
It is within and I can see it before me,
A beautiful array of colourful light illuminated beautiful movements.
They whirled, stormed, breathed, curled, combusted, collapsed, and
convulsed in the distance –
A fire did burn, upon that stage,
Burning in flames so expressive, so churning with life and soul, that
it seems as though his whole world would never be the same.

Writing to Benjamin Francis Leftwich's song *1904*

I feel so alive... gentle pressure on my chest from the inside beats.
The love is gently floating, spreading out into the air, this moment-
so full of euphoria that beautiful pictures arise. I can't stop writing
these typewriter words, as words become gold, with glimmering
soft golden light... my ears... this music... this song born of heaven-
sheds rays of multicolored shine from earthly speakers... it speaks...
I want to speak. This is what I want to do... To bring people together,
hearts strung and joined by the love of love, the ultimate connection,
and its meanings... Multilayered gems on the roads of life... The
scarves of life floating, and gleaming in the summer light... Flying as
the flight path of dreams... ours with time...

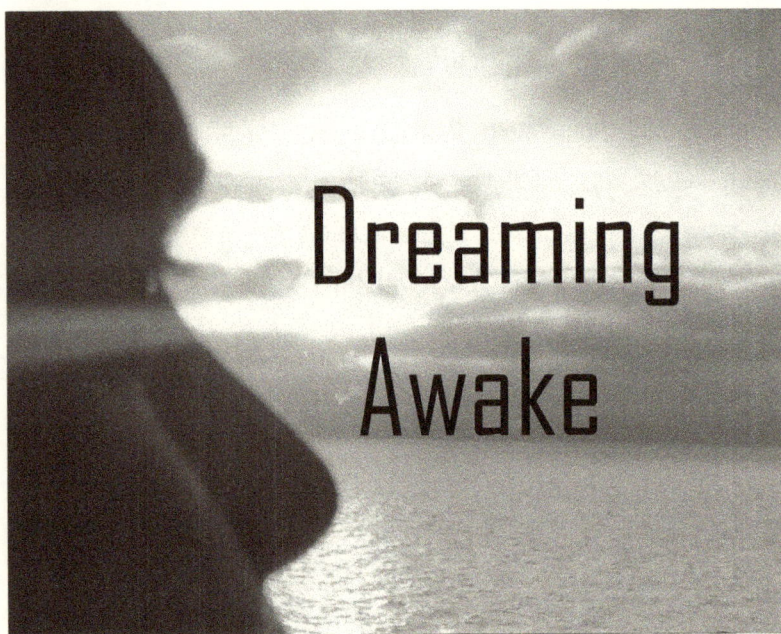

Dreaming Awake

The What Was, What Is, and What Will Be

What comes to mind...?
Our names,
This place,
These dreams,
And that amazing opportunity to be one.

In my mind...
I'm reeling a sequence of events like a filmstrip:
Scratchy, square images flash before my eyes,
All colors, shapes, and sounds,
Are pleasing to this heart.

I want to hold them,
Breathe them,
And revisit them in the future,
To experience the magic of being new.

Those first-time loves...
First time singing with guitar,
First time gazing at midnight stars,
First time realizing, my purpose in life... and how to live it.

This spark,
This heartfelt ember:

SARAH LEO

Litters my inner world,
Fireworks springing from
Action, intention, and dreams...
Those sweet immediate dreams... I look forward to reaching them
So that one day, my life will be fulfilled.

I once read a quote that went something along the lines,
The date you were born, and the year that you pass...
Mean nothing at all...
It's the little dash in the middle that counts.

I wish to use every split-second moment
In this exceedingly beautiful way...
To appreciate life's gifts...
Bitter and sweet:
To use my deepest passions...
Following my heart's desire:
And to manifest those dreams...
Never losing sight of their significance...
So that 80 years from now,
My life will *mirror* a meant to be path.

Crossroads Intertwined and Aligned by Music

That instant moment...
When the stars seem aligned...

.

Where signs,
Show you the way...
And coincidence seems too perfect, to be just that...

Details, remnants, traces of the meant-to-be
Are trailing from your stride...
There's something about your presence that calls to the road I'm
on...
That highway of dreams, intersections of decision...
Seems like you've been a passenger, for a long time...
How am I seeing you now, for the first time?

Those moments...
When even a *few* of your words make everything align:
In harmony, *in* tune, & *in*-depth with familiarity...
– Is it your voice?
The way you lay down your pride to ask the right questions?
Maybe I've seen you before...
Somewhere familiar?

I want to ask... because I'm curious to know,
Were our paths rerouted to cross?
With a lightning bolt of directing.
Whoever it was,
– *Thank you* for the link.

Bird flights in sync, moving with momentum,
I'm excited to enjoy this ride.
The simplicity of time spent,
Talking into the night with timeless stars as our witness,
These are beautiful, subtle moments I wouldn't trade for the world...

You are the voice of R&B, Soul, and Jazz...
With a spark that defines the dream, a passion to stride through doors,
And a confidence... *rooted* in ease to get you there...

These words describe our paths,
Tracks merging towards...
In a remarkable way.

The Doors

A steel set of doors,
Wedged together with rigid authority.
Four in total,
And on each of the halves:
"PUSH TO EXIT" reads,
In red engraved on black.
Decisively in the middle of each unit,
Claiming precision in abiding self-made laws,
Almost to say: "Just try to pull... see what happens."

But daring is what we need...
To be, emit, transmit and exit through to new horizons, honored
memories,
And self-made signs,
Guiding your new, more authentic route.
If you want to go far,
Pass through self-made doors,
Give it your all.
Push for the things you deserve...
And keep moving forward.
These doors are old, yet still in silver hue
Old yet new,
Your door is timeless...
Just a few fingerprints on the glass exist...
But in order to leave your mark
And let the world know who came...
Finger prints are necessary...
As I "PUSH TO EXIT"... I don't look back.

Recollection of Lines

Snippets of life,
Gathering speed,
Flashing before my eyes... momentum building like a linear race...

I recall the smell of bread homemade,

SARAH LEO

Wafting through a warm, sunlit kitchen,
With my grandma's voice, speaking Italian in the background...
Spinning lines remembering an older country, a life among wheat
fields a long time ago...
Memory leaping and rushing near...

I've got markers in my hand...washable yet staining wet...
And suddenly, they race in rapid lines,
Both left then right:
In brightly colored hue...
Excited for more,
I continue along these lines,
Absorbed by my geometric rainbow....

These *moments* string together in my mind...
Like sheets of fabric, draping along clotheslines of Italy
A brightly colored network,
From a window to the next:
Directly across... very near, very shared and very connected, in a
beautiful way...
These two-dimensional shapes start to dance...
Blowing in the wind.
Some fly away... some hang on like lost lovers found.
I hold it, holding on, and skip to more scenes.
The last one, the last mental slide-show before sleep takes place
with stars...

Connected by imaginary lines which cast me in wonder
The constellations, outside my bedroom window mark,
White silver moonlight, streaming through the blinds...
They made lines like the sheet of paper I transferred these
thoughts...
I was six, and I still remember how shaky letters morphed into
handwriting swirls...

Over the years,
Line connections *grew* ....
Connecting to amazing people...
Brilliantly honest souls, who you knew you could count on:
Included once again...
The *brave and scared,*
Led courageous gestures of love, helping the other...
Collecting school books dropped amongst laughter in the hall.
These people – and moments – are strung together by memory:
The lines inside my room from the moon,
The material that fascinated my heart in Italy,
And the track of life, bringing me closer to you...
Remember when we wrote our new script lines ...?
The ones we chose to write...
Every line gave me joy.

The Dignity I Feel

For the first time, I love the skin I'm in ... all of its laugh lines, beauty marks, and scars tell my story...
A story where pages, how they move from one chapter to the next, start to merge...
I can flow across any stage with ease, giving slow and steady gestures to the sky,
Grounded in strength and authenticity...
This perspective...
Makes me glow, flush, shine with yellow light from within reaching out.
This is who I am today...
I can feel rain... I get to feel rain, and if I want to dance in it, I can.
The dignity I feel from being true... is like a burden off my shoulders... nothing to fear but fear itself replays
And my passion for life can break free like the birds out of a cage.
Because of you...

You've kissed my skin so gently... the pain went away where thoughts inflicted damage.
"Your eyes, to see the beauty you possess, on the inside too...
Your smile to show the world inner happiness creates more...
And your hands, to hold trust, and reach to the ones you love."

Even when you feel small, you are still a blessing to others.

Like a piece in the great mosaic of life...

Blowing in the wind, my eyes set deep at the rush and pull of the rolling tide.
A calmness washes over, when I think of the dignity I feel...

Formula Poem 1

Stone hard work.
Stone hard experimentation.
Stone hard faith in capability.
[Inspiration's secret]

Formula Poem 2

Water, it flows like this reverie
Water, my mind like a glimmering fountain
Water, hoping it flows into a stream of connection.
[What we need]

The Call and Most Immediate Arrow

What if God suddenly called?... One thing's for sure, I can say that it would be one of the most profound experiences... but what would you say? It would be good to converse, and just talk about life, nature's gallery that is the outdoors, and the fascinating people He made in all of our perfect imperfections, walking around the Earth searching for something meaningful... I'd ask if inspiration surrounds, and that I think we need each other. We're all connected to each other and are drawn on the basis of needing to authentically say or do... How about the law of attraction? That unique, wonderful and somewhat terrifying idea. But is it what you want or what you need that is attracted to you?... I'd ask him that. I picture multicolored arrows, personalized to our story and life: growing, twisting and turning left, right, between buildings, through fields, beyond all hallways, doors, avenues and moments of chance... Is it those very arrows of direction that we're following? A path set out before our time, paved in things we need to see and hear to become? Like routes of an interconnected subway station. I want to think that life is constantly being merged with non-coincidental stops to better ourselves... to become our best selves... So that when we feel happy, we're on the path to both enlightenment and simplicity in all its beauty; but when we feel frustrated, we go against grains of salt and sparks from screeching trains... I believe we are meant to choose a path to find peace for ourselves and others. Discordia is a sign post telling you "wrong way"... in that you are needed and valued somewhere else. When you recognize this call to disembark and take this unintended detour, when your act on the wings of faith for something new... It brings you back on highways seeking change, speeding faster in the direction of where we were meant to experience, and be a living, breathing testament of what success, health and happiness looks like for you.

The Intensity of Now

We live in a beautiful world, a community of outstanding individuals... striving for personal excellence. In this way, we exist for our dreams. We envision this life of hope from familiar thoughts, and beautiful images of mind. You are everything and more than your expectations and anything is possible if you run that mile with grace. Once you make the decision, you know where paths of life and maps of your future can evolve. A conceptual arrow of movement will point your way, leading footsteps to another adventure, another chapter and another breathtaking moment you seek. When you deny fear and crave finish lines, you will feel it in your heart. You were born for this track and deserve nothing less than what makes your soul happy.

Fascination Anticipation

Flights intertwined,
Fates realigned,
Signs shown from behind,
Unknown fascination lives...
Anticipation warms every lightning fierce storm.
Diamond studded skies,
Bittersweet lies,
And midnight lullabies,
Remind me of you...

SARAH LEO

Childhood dreams
Conflicting inner screams
For pent up dreaming awake.
Visions repeat,
Of everything I want and need to be,
Dusty travels,
And whispering winds unravel,
Our grain of salt philosophy.
Destinations unknown
Expose reflections of our hearts evolution...
An upward push to the electric fast reach
For speeding self-worth
Resulting in all knowing thanks.
Your heart is craving for thoughts,
Fueled by passion
Unlimited and timeless...
Ready to live this life
Projecting and stepping into reality,
That every part of your
Beautifully,
Irreplaceable,
Soul,
Matters.
Stay true and believe in the power of you.